50 Premium French Dishes for Home

By: Kelly Johnson

Table of Contents

- Coq au Vin
- Beef Bourguignon
- Duck Confit
- Bouillabaisse
- Sole Meunière
- Quiche Lorraine
- Ratatouille
- Escargots de Bourgogne
- Croque Monsieur
- Pâté en Croûte
- Tarte Tatin
- Foie Gras
- Cassoulet
- Chateaubriand
- Gratin Dauphinois
- French Onion Soup
- Salade Niçoise
- Tarte aux Fruits
- Magret de Canard
- Bœuf à la Mode
- Fois Gras Torchon
- Soupe au Pistou
- Poulet Rôti
- Moules Marinières
- Bouchees à la Reine
- Pommes Anna
- Cordon Bleu
- Salade de Chèvre Chaud
- Salade Lyonnaise
- Chou Farci
- Blanquette de Veau
- Entrecôte Bordelaise
- Pâtisserie Mille-Feuille
- Crêpes Suzette
- Crème Brûlée

- Pot-au-Feu
- Hachis Parmentier
- Cassoulet Toulousain
- Pâté de Campagne
- Salade de Foie de Volaille
- Gratin de Courgettes
- Oeufs en Cocotte
- Tarte Flambée
- Vichyssoise
- Soufflé au Fromage
- Salade de Langoustines
- Brandade de Morue
- Gâteau Basque
- Pain Complet
- Pain de Campagne

Coq au Vin (France)

Ingredients:

- 1 whole chicken, cut into pieces
- 1 bottle red wine (Burgundy or Pinot Noir)
- 2 tbsp olive oil
- 1 onion, chopped
- 2 carrots, peeled and chopped
- 2 cloves garlic, minced
- 2 cups chicken broth
- 2 tbsp tomato paste
- 1 bay leaf
- 2 tsp thyme
- 1/2 lb mushrooms, sliced
- 1/2 lb small pearl onions, peeled
- 4 oz bacon, diced
- Salt and pepper to taste

Instructions:

1. In a large pot or Dutch oven, heat olive oil over medium heat. Brown the chicken pieces on all sides and remove from the pot.
2. In the same pot, add the bacon and cook until crisp. Add the onions, carrots, and garlic, cooking until softened, about 5 minutes.
3. Stir in the tomato paste, then return the chicken to the pot. Pour in the wine and chicken broth, add the bay leaf and thyme, and season with salt and pepper.
4. Bring to a simmer, cover, and cook for 1.5-2 hours, until the chicken is tender.
5. In a separate pan, sauté the mushrooms and pearl onions until golden. Add them to the pot in the final 15 minutes of cooking.
6. Remove the chicken pieces and reduce the sauce if needed. Serve the chicken with the vegetables and sauce.

Beef Bourguignon (France)

Ingredients:

- 2 lbs beef chuck, cut into 2-inch cubes
- 1 bottle red wine (Burgundy or Pinot Noir)
- 2 cups beef broth
- 1 onion, chopped
- 2 carrots, peeled and chopped
- 2 cloves garlic, minced
- 2 tbsp tomato paste
- 1 bay leaf
- 2 tsp thyme
- 1/2 lb small pearl onions, peeled
- 1/2 lb mushrooms, sliced
- 4 oz bacon, diced
- Salt and pepper to taste

Instructions:

1. In a large Dutch oven, brown the beef cubes in batches with a little olive oil. Remove and set aside.
2. In the same pot, cook the bacon until crispy. Add the onion, carrots, and garlic and sauté until softened, about 5 minutes.
3. Stir in the tomato paste, then return the beef to the pot. Pour in the wine and beef broth, add the bay leaf and thyme, and season with salt and pepper.
4. Bring to a simmer, cover, and cook for 2-3 hours, until the beef is tender.
5. Sauté the mushrooms and pearl onions separately, then add them to the pot in the last 30 minutes of cooking.
6. Serve the stew with crusty bread or over mashed potatoes.

Duck Confit (France)

Ingredients:

- 4 duck legs, bone-in
- 4 cups duck fat (or a mix of olive oil and butter)
- 4 garlic cloves, smashed
- 2 sprigs thyme
- 1 bay leaf
- Salt and pepper to taste

Instructions:

1. Season the duck legs with salt and pepper. Place them in a baking dish with garlic, thyme, and bay leaf.
2. Pour the duck fat over the legs, ensuring they are fully submerged. Cover with foil and cook in a preheated oven at 275°F (135°C) for 2-3 hours, until the duck is very tender.
3. Once cooked, remove the duck legs and crisp them in a hot skillet with a little duck fat for 5-7 minutes on each side.
4. Serve the duck confit with potatoes or a simple salad.

Bouillabaisse (France)

Ingredients:

- 1 lb firm white fish (e.g., cod, snapper), cut into pieces
- 1/2 lb shellfish (mussels, clams, shrimp)
- 2 tbsp olive oil
- 1 onion, chopped
- 2 cloves garlic, minced
- 1 leek, sliced
- 2 tomatoes, chopped
- 1/2 cup white wine
- 4 cups fish stock
- 1/2 tsp saffron threads
- 1 bay leaf
- 1 tsp thyme
- Salt and pepper to taste
- Fresh parsley, chopped
- Rouille sauce (optional)

Instructions:

1. Heat olive oil in a large pot over medium heat. Sauté the onion, garlic, and leek until softened, about 5 minutes.
2. Add the tomatoes, wine, and fish stock, and bring to a simmer. Add the saffron, bay leaf, thyme, salt, and pepper.
3. Simmer for 20 minutes, then add the fish and shellfish. Cook for an additional 10 minutes, until the fish is cooked through and the shellfish has opened.
4. Serve the bouillabaisse with a drizzle of rouille sauce and a sprinkle of fresh parsley.

Sole Meunière (France)

Ingredients:

- 4 sole fillets (or other white fish)
- 1/4 cup all-purpose flour
- 4 tbsp butter
- 1/4 cup white wine
- 2 tbsp lemon juice
- Fresh parsley, chopped
- Salt and pepper to taste

Instructions:

1. Dredge the sole fillets in flour, shaking off the excess.
2. In a large skillet, melt 2 tbsp of butter over medium-high heat. Add the fillets and cook for 2-3 minutes per side until golden and cooked through. Remove the fillets and set aside.
3. In the same skillet, add the remaining butter, white wine, and lemon juice. Cook for 2-3 minutes, allowing the sauce to reduce.
4. Pour the sauce over the fish and garnish with fresh parsley. Serve immediately.

Quiche Lorraine (France)

Ingredients for Crust:

- 1 1/4 cups all-purpose flour
- 1/2 tsp salt
- 1/2 cup cold unsalted butter, cubed
- 2-3 tbsp cold water

Ingredients for Filling:

- 6 large eggs
- 1 1/2 cups heavy cream
- 1 cup grated Gruyère cheese
- 1/2 cup cooked bacon, crumbled
- 1/2 cup chopped onion (optional)
- Salt and pepper to taste

Instructions:

1. Preheat the oven to 375°F (190°C). For the crust, combine flour and salt in a food processor. Add butter and pulse until the mixture resembles coarse crumbs. Gradually add water until the dough comes together.
2. Roll the dough out on a floured surface and fit it into a tart pan. Prick the bottom with a fork and bake for 10-12 minutes until lightly golden.
3. For the filling, whisk together the eggs and cream. Stir in the cheese, bacon, onion (if using), salt, and pepper.
4. Pour the filling into the crust and bake for 30-35 minutes, until the quiche is set and lightly browned on top.
5. Allow to cool for a few minutes before slicing. Serve warm or at room temperature.

Ratatouille (France)

Ingredients:

- 1 eggplant, sliced
- 1 zucchini, sliced
- 1 yellow bell pepper, chopped
- 1 onion, chopped
- 2 tomatoes, chopped
- 2 cloves garlic, minced
- 2 tbsp olive oil
- 1 tsp thyme
- Salt and pepper to taste

Instructions:

1. Heat olive oil in a large skillet over medium heat. Add the onion, garlic, and bell pepper and cook until softened, about 5 minutes.
2. Add the eggplant, zucchini, and tomatoes, and cook for an additional 10-15 minutes until the vegetables are tender.
3. Stir in the thyme, season with salt and pepper, and cook for another 5 minutes.
4. Serve the ratatouille warm, as a side dish or main course with crusty bread.

Escargots de Bourgogne (France)

Ingredients:

- 24 escargots (snails), shelled and cleaned
- 1/2 cup unsalted butter, softened
- 4 cloves garlic, minced
- 1/4 cup fresh parsley, chopped
- 2 tbsp white wine
- 1 tbsp lemon juice
- Salt and pepper to taste

Instructions:

1. Preheat the oven to 375°F (190°C). In a bowl, combine the butter, garlic, parsley, white wine, lemon juice, salt, and pepper.
2. Place the escargots in their shells or in a baking dish. Fill each escargot shell with the garlic butter mixture.
3. Bake for 12-15 minutes until the butter is bubbling and the snails are heated through.
4. Serve hot with crusty French bread to soak up the garlic butter.

Croque Monsieur (France)

Ingredients:

- 8 slices of white bread
- 4 slices of ham
- 1 1/2 cups Gruyère cheese, grated
- 1/4 cup Dijon mustard
- 1 tbsp butter
- 1 tbsp flour
- 1 cup whole milk
- Salt and pepper to taste
- Fresh parsley (optional, for garnish)

Instructions:

1. Preheat the oven to 375°F (190°C).
2. In a small saucepan, melt the butter over medium heat. Add the flour and whisk for 1-2 minutes to make a roux. Gradually add the milk while whisking constantly. Cook until the sauce thickens, about 5-7 minutes. Season with salt and pepper.
3. Spread mustard on each slice of bread. Place a slice of ham on four of the slices, followed by a generous portion of grated Gruyère cheese.
4. Top with the remaining bread slices, then spread the béchamel sauce on top of each sandwich.
5. Sprinkle the remaining cheese over the béchamel, then bake for 10-15 minutes until golden brown and bubbly. Serve immediately, garnished with fresh parsley if desired.

Pâté en Croûte (France)

Ingredients:

- 1 lb ground pork
- 1/2 lb ground veal
- 1/4 lb chicken liver, cleaned and chopped
- 1/2 cup foie gras (optional, for a richer filling)
- 1/4 cup brandy or cognac
- 1 onion, finely chopped
- 2 cloves garlic, minced
- 1/4 tsp thyme
- 1/4 tsp allspice
- 1/4 tsp black pepper
- Salt to taste
- 1 sheet puff pastry
- 1 egg (for egg wash)

Instructions:

1. Preheat the oven to 375°F (190°C).
2. In a skillet, sauté the onion and garlic until soft. Add the chicken liver, cooking until browned, then deglaze with brandy or cognac. Allow to cool.
3. In a large bowl, mix the ground pork, veal, and foie gras with the sautéed liver and onions. Add thyme, allspice, pepper, and salt. Mix until well combined.
4. Roll out the puff pastry and place it in a loaf pan, leaving extra pastry hanging over the edges.
5. Spoon the meat mixture into the pastry-lined pan, packing it tightly.
6. Fold the excess pastry over the top to seal. Brush with egg wash.
7. Bake for 45-50 minutes until golden brown and fully cooked. Let it rest before slicing and serving.

Tarte Tatin (France)

Ingredients:

- 6-8 apples (preferably Granny Smith or Golden Delicious)
- 1/2 cup butter
- 1 cup sugar
- 1 sheet puff pastry
- 1 tbsp lemon juice
- Pinch of salt

Instructions:

1. Preheat the oven to 375°F (190°C).
2. In a heavy skillet, melt the butter over medium heat. Add the sugar and cook until it turns golden brown, forming a caramel.
3. Peel, core, and slice the apples. Arrange them in a circular pattern in the skillet over the caramel, then drizzle with lemon juice and sprinkle with a pinch of salt. Cook for 10-15 minutes until the apples begin to soften.
4. Roll the puff pastry to fit the skillet and cover the apples. Tuck the edges inside the pan.
5. Bake for 25-30 minutes, until the pastry is golden and puffed.
6. Allow the tart to cool slightly before carefully inverting it onto a serving platter. Serve warm.

Foie Gras (France)

Ingredients:

- 1 lb foie gras (duck or goose liver)
- Salt and pepper to taste
- 1 tbsp cognac or brandy
- 1 tbsp butter
- Fresh herbs (thyme, rosemary) for garnish

Instructions:

1. Preheat the oven to 300°F (150°C).
2. Season the foie gras generously with salt and pepper.
3. Heat butter in an ovenproof skillet over medium heat. Sear the foie gras on each side for 2-3 minutes until golden brown.
4. Add cognac or brandy and allow it to flambe or cook off the alcohol.
5. Transfer the skillet to the oven and bake for 10-15 minutes, depending on desired doneness (foie gras is best served slightly rare inside).
6. Serve immediately with fresh herbs and toasted baguette slices.

Cassoulet (France)

Ingredients:

- 1 lb white beans (like cannellini or great northern)
- 1 lb pork shoulder, cut into chunks
- 1/2 lb sausage (Toulouse or other garlic sausage), sliced
- 4 slices bacon, chopped
- 1 onion, chopped
- 2 carrots, peeled and chopped
- 4 cloves garlic, minced
- 2 cups chicken broth
- 1 bay leaf
- 2 sprigs thyme
- Salt and pepper to taste
- Fresh parsley for garnish

Instructions:

1. Preheat the oven to 325°F (165°C).
2. Soak the beans overnight in water, then drain and set aside.
3. In a large Dutch oven, cook the bacon over medium heat until crispy. Remove and set aside.
4. Brown the pork and sausage in the bacon fat. Remove and set aside.
5. In the same pot, sauté the onion, carrots, and garlic until softened. Add the beans, meats, chicken broth, bay leaf, and thyme. Season with salt and pepper.
6. Bring to a boil, then reduce the heat and simmer for 2 hours until the beans are tender.
7. Sprinkle fresh parsley over the cassoulet before serving.

Chateaubriand (France)

Ingredients:

- 2 lbs center-cut beef tenderloin (Chateaubriand cut)
- 2 tbsp olive oil
- 4 tbsp butter
- 2 cloves garlic, minced
- 2 sprigs thyme
- Salt and pepper to taste

Instructions:

1. Preheat the oven to 400°F (200°C).
2. Season the beef with salt and pepper.
3. Heat olive oil in a large skillet over medium-high heat. Sear the beef on all sides until browned.
4. Transfer the beef to a roasting pan and roast for 25-30 minutes for medium-rare.
5. While the beef is roasting, melt butter in the skillet and sauté the garlic and thyme for 1-2 minutes.
6. Remove the beef from the oven and let it rest for 10 minutes before slicing.
7. Serve with the garlic-thyme butter and your choice of side dishes.

Gratin Dauphinois (France)

Ingredients:

- 2 lbs potatoes, peeled and thinly sliced
- 2 cups heavy cream
- 1 cup milk
- 2 cloves garlic, minced
- 1 tbsp butter
- 1 cup grated Gruyère cheese
- Salt and pepper to taste

Instructions:

1. Preheat the oven to 375°F (190°C).
2. In a saucepan, combine cream, milk, garlic, butter, salt, and pepper. Heat until it begins to simmer.
3. In a buttered baking dish, layer the potato slices and pour the cream mixture over them. Sprinkle cheese between layers and on top.
4. Cover with foil and bake for 45 minutes. Remove the foil and bake for an additional 20-30 minutes until golden and bubbly.
5. Let it rest for 10 minutes before serving.

French Onion Soup (France)

Ingredients:

- 4 large onions, thinly sliced
- 2 tbsp butter
- 2 tbsp olive oil
- 1 tsp thyme
- 1 bay leaf
- 1/2 cup dry white wine
- 4 cups beef broth
- 1 baguette, sliced
- 2 cups grated Gruyère cheese

Instructions:

1. In a large pot, melt butter and olive oil over medium heat. Add onions and cook, stirring occasionally, for 40-45 minutes until golden and caramelized.
2. Add thyme and bay leaf, then deglaze with white wine. Cook for another 5 minutes.
3. Pour in the beef broth and bring to a simmer for 20 minutes. Season with salt and pepper to taste.
4. Toast the baguette slices. Ladle the soup into bowls, top with the toasted bread, and sprinkle with Gruyère cheese.
5. Place the bowls under a broiler for 2-3 minutes until the cheese melts and is bubbly. Serve immediately.

Salade Niçoise (France)

Ingredients:

- 4 cups mixed lettuce greens
- 1/2 lb green beans, blanched
- 4 hard-boiled eggs, halved
- 2 medium tomatoes, cut into wedges
- 1/2 cup Kalamata olives
- 1/2 lb tuna (canned in olive oil or grilled)
- 2 tbsp olive oil
- 1 tbsp red wine vinegar
- 1 tsp Dijon mustard
- Salt and pepper to taste

Instructions:

1. In a large salad bowl, arrange the lettuce greens. Top with the green beans, eggs, tomatoes, olives, and tuna.
2. Whisk together olive oil, red wine vinegar, Dijon mustard, salt, and pepper to make the dressing.
3. Drizzle the dressing over the salad and toss gently. Serve immediately.

Tarte aux Fruits (Fruit Tart)

Ingredients:

- 1 pre-baked tart shell (about 9 inches)
- 1 cup pastry cream (see recipe below)
- 2 cups mixed fresh fruit (such as strawberries, blueberries, kiwi, and raspberries)
- 1/4 cup apricot jam (for glaze)

Pastry Cream:

- 1 cup whole milk
- 2 large egg yolks
- 1/4 cup sugar
- 2 tbsp cornstarch
- 1 tsp vanilla extract
- 2 tbsp butter

Instructions:

1. For the pastry cream: In a saucepan, heat the milk until just simmering. In a bowl, whisk the egg yolks with sugar and cornstarch until smooth. Gradually add the hot milk to the egg mixture while whisking constantly.
2. Pour the mixture back into the saucepan and cook over medium heat until it thickens, about 2-3 minutes. Stir in the vanilla extract and butter. Remove from heat and let cool completely.
3. Spread the cooled pastry cream evenly into the pre-baked tart shell.
4. Arrange the mixed fresh fruit on top of the pastry cream in a decorative pattern.
5. To glaze, heat the apricot jam in a small saucepan until it becomes liquid. Brush the glaze over the fruit to give it a shiny finish.
6. Chill the tart in the refrigerator for at least 1 hour before serving.

Magret de Canard (Duck Breast)

Ingredients:

- 2 duck breasts (magret de canard)
- Salt and pepper to taste
- 1 tbsp vegetable oil
- 1/4 cup red wine
- 1 tbsp balsamic vinegar
- 1 tbsp honey
- Fresh thyme (for garnish)

Instructions:

1. Score the fat of the duck breasts in a crisscross pattern. Season both sides with salt and pepper.
2. Heat vegetable oil in a skillet over medium-high heat. Place the duck breasts fat-side down and sear for 6-8 minutes until the fat is crispy and golden brown.
3. Flip the duck breasts and cook for an additional 4-5 minutes for medium-rare or longer if preferred.
4. Remove the duck breasts from the skillet and let rest for 5 minutes.
5. In the same skillet, add red wine, balsamic vinegar, and honey. Bring to a simmer and cook for 3-5 minutes, until the sauce reduces and thickens slightly.
6. Slice the duck breasts thinly and drizzle the sauce over the top. Garnish with fresh thyme and serve.

Bœuf à la Mode (Beef Braised in Wine)

Ingredients:

- 3 lbs beef chuck roast
- 2 tbsp olive oil
- 1 onion, chopped
- 2 carrots, peeled and chopped
- 2 cloves garlic, minced
- 2 cups red wine
- 2 cups beef broth
- 1 bouquet garni (thyme, bay leaf, parsley)
- Salt and pepper to taste
- 1 tbsp butter

Instructions:

1. Preheat the oven to 325°F (160°C).
2. In a large oven-safe pot, heat olive oil over medium-high heat. Brown the beef roast on all sides, about 10 minutes. Remove and set aside.
3. In the same pot, sauté the onion, carrots, and garlic for 5 minutes until softened.
4. Add red wine, beef broth, and bouquet garni. Stir well, then return the beef to the pot. Season with salt and pepper.
5. Cover the pot and braise in the oven for 3 hours, or until the meat is tender and easily shreds with a fork.
6. Remove the beef from the pot and let it rest. Discard the bouquet garni. Melt butter into the sauce and serve with the sliced beef.

Foie Gras Torchon (Foie Gras in a Cloth)

Ingredients:

- 1 lb foie gras (duck or goose liver)
- 1/4 cup cognac or Armagnac
- 1 tbsp salt
- 1/2 tbsp white pepper
- 1/2 tbsp sugar
- 1/4 tsp quatre-épices (French spice mix)
- Cheesecloth

Instructions:

1. Clean the foie gras, removing any veins. Season with salt, pepper, sugar, and quatre-épices.
2. Place the foie gras in a shallow dish and pour over the cognac. Let it marinate for 2 hours at room temperature.
3. After marinating, roll the foie gras in a cheesecloth, shaping it into a log.
4. Tie the ends of the cheesecloth tightly and poach the foie gras in simmering water for 45 minutes.
5. Chill the foie gras in the refrigerator for at least 6 hours before serving. Slice and serve with toasted baguette.

Soupe au Pistou (Provençal Vegetable Soup with Pesto)

Ingredients:

- 1 onion, chopped
- 2 carrots, peeled and chopped
- 1 zucchini, chopped
- 1 potato, peeled and chopped
- 1 cup green beans, chopped
- 4 cups vegetable broth
- 2 tbsp olive oil
- Salt and pepper to taste

Pistou:

- 1 cup fresh basil leaves
- 2 cloves garlic
- 1/4 cup olive oil
- 1/4 cup grated Parmesan cheese

Instructions:

1. In a large pot, heat olive oil over medium heat. Add onion, carrots, zucchini, potato, and green beans. Sauté for 5 minutes until slightly softened.
2. Add vegetable broth, salt, and pepper. Bring to a boil, then reduce to a simmer and cook for 20 minutes, until the vegetables are tender.
3. While the soup simmers, make the pistou. In a food processor, blend the basil, garlic, olive oil, and Parmesan cheese until smooth.
4. Stir the pistou into the soup just before serving. Ladle into bowls and serve with crusty bread.

Poulet Rôti (Roast Chicken)

Ingredients:

- 1 whole chicken (about 4 lbs)
- 2 tbsp olive oil
- 1 lemon, halved
- 4 garlic cloves, smashed
- Fresh herbs (thyme, rosemary)
- Salt and pepper to taste

Instructions:

1. Preheat the oven to 375°F (190°C).
2. Season the chicken inside and out with salt and pepper. Stuff the cavity with lemon halves, garlic, and fresh herbs.
3. Rub the chicken with olive oil and place it on a roasting pan.
4. Roast for 1 hour and 20 minutes, or until the chicken reaches an internal temperature of 165°F (75°C).
5. Let the chicken rest for 10 minutes before carving and serving.

Moules Marinières (Mussels in White Wine)

Ingredients:

- 2 lbs fresh mussels, cleaned and debearded
- 1 onion, chopped
- 2 cloves garlic, minced
- 1 cup white wine
- 2 tbsp butter
- 1/4 cup fresh parsley, chopped
- Salt and pepper to taste

Instructions:

1. In a large pot, melt butter over medium heat. Add onion and garlic, cooking for 3-4 minutes until softened.
2. Add the mussels and white wine. Cover and cook for 5-7 minutes until the mussels have opened.
3. Season with salt, pepper, and fresh parsley. Serve immediately with crusty bread.

Bouchées à la Reine (Puff Pastry with Creamy Chicken Filling)

Ingredients:

- 4 puff pastry shells (store-bought or homemade)
- 1/2 lb chicken breast, cooked and diced
- 1/2 cup mushrooms, sliced
- 1/4 cup butter
- 1/4 cup flour
- 1 cup chicken broth
- 1/2 cup heavy cream
- Salt and pepper to taste

Instructions:

1. Preheat the oven to 375°F (190°C). Bake the puff pastry shells according to the package instructions, then set aside.
2. In a skillet, melt butter over medium heat. Add mushrooms and cook until softened.
3. Stir in the flour to make a roux, then gradually add the chicken broth, whisking constantly.
4. Add the cream and cooked chicken. Stir until thickened and season with salt and pepper.
5. Fill the puff pastry shells with the chicken mixture and serve immediately.

Pommes Anna (Potatoes Anna)

Ingredients:

- 2 lbs potatoes, peeled and thinly sliced
- 1/4 cup butter, melted
- Salt and pepper to taste
- Fresh thyme (optional)

Instructions:

1. Preheat the oven to 400°F (200°C).
2. Grease a baking dish with some of the melted butter. Layer the potato slices in the dish, slightly overlapping each slice. Season with salt and pepper between each layer.
3. Drizzle the remaining butter over the top and sprinkle with fresh thyme if using.
4. Cover with foil and bake for 45 minutes. Remove the foil and bake for another 20 minutes until the potatoes are tender and golden.
5. Allow to cool for a few minutes before serving.

Cordon Bleu (Chicken or Veal)

Ingredients:

- 4 boneless chicken breasts (or veal)
- 4 slices ham
- 4 slices Gruyère cheese
- 1 cup flour
- 2 eggs, beaten
- 1 cup breadcrumbs
- Salt and pepper to taste
- Vegetable oil for frying
- 1 tbsp butter (optional)

Instructions:

1. Preheat your oven to 375°F (190°C).
2. Place each chicken breast (or veal) between two sheets of plastic wrap and pound to an even thickness (about 1/4 inch thick).
3. Lay a slice of ham and cheese on each breast. Fold the edges over and secure with toothpicks.
4. Dredge each piece in flour, dip in beaten eggs, and then coat in breadcrumbs.
5. Heat vegetable oil in a large skillet over medium-high heat. Fry each Cordon Bleu for 4-5 minutes per side, until golden brown.
6. Transfer the chicken (or veal) to a baking sheet and bake for 10-12 minutes to ensure the cheese is melted and the meat is fully cooked.
7. Remove toothpicks and serve immediately.

Salade de Chèvre Chaud (Warm Goat Cheese Salad)

Ingredients:

- 4 slices goat cheese (on a log)
- 1 tbsp olive oil
- 1 tbsp honey
- 1 tbsp fresh thyme, chopped
- 4 cups mixed salad greens (e.g., arugula, spinach, frisée)
- 1/4 cup walnuts, toasted
- 1/4 cup balsamic vinegar
- Salt and pepper to taste

Instructions:

1. Preheat the oven to 350°F (175°C). Place the slices of goat cheese on a baking sheet lined with parchment paper. Drizzle with olive oil and honey, then sprinkle with thyme.
2. Bake for 5-7 minutes, or until the cheese is soft and golden on top.
3. While the cheese bakes, toss the salad greens with balsamic vinegar, olive oil, salt, and pepper.
4. Arrange the greens on a plate, then top with the warm goat cheese and toasted walnuts.
5. Serve immediately, drizzling any extra honey and olive oil over the top.

Salade Lyonnaise

Ingredients:

- 4 cups frisée lettuce, torn into pieces
- 1/2 cup bacon lardons (or pancetta)
- 2 eggs
- 1/4 cup red wine vinegar
- 1 tbsp Dijon mustard
- 2 tbsp olive oil
- Salt and pepper to taste
- 1 tbsp fresh parsley, chopped

Instructions:

1. Cook the bacon lardons in a skillet over medium heat until crispy, about 5-7 minutes. Remove from the pan and set aside.
2. In the same skillet, fry the eggs sunny side up or poach them. Season with salt and pepper.
3. In a small bowl, whisk together red wine vinegar, mustard, olive oil, salt, and pepper to make the dressing.
4. Toss the frisée lettuce with the bacon lardons and the dressing.
5. Plate the salad and top with the fried or poached egg. Garnish with fresh parsley and serve immediately.

Chou Farci (Stuffed Cabbage)

Ingredients:

- 1 large head of cabbage
- 1 lb ground pork
- 1/2 lb ground beef
- 1/2 cup cooked rice
- 1 onion, chopped
- 2 cloves garlic, minced
- 1 egg
- 1/4 cup fresh parsley, chopped
- 2 cups tomato sauce
- 1 tsp thyme
- Salt and pepper to taste

Instructions:

1. Bring a large pot of water to a boil. Carefully remove the leaves from the cabbage and blanch them for 2-3 minutes until softened. Drain and set aside.
2. In a skillet, sauté the onion and garlic in olive oil until soft, about 5 minutes. Let cool.
3. In a bowl, combine the ground pork, beef, rice, egg, parsley, sautéed onion, garlic, thyme, salt, and pepper.
4. Place a small amount of filling in the center of each cabbage leaf and roll them up tightly, folding in the sides as you go.
5. In a large pot, layer the stuffed cabbage rolls. Pour the tomato sauce over the rolls, cover, and simmer for 1-1.5 hours, until the cabbage is tender and the filling is cooked through.
6. Serve hot with a drizzle of sauce.

Blanquette de Veau (Veal Stew)

Ingredients:

- 2 lbs veal stew meat, cut into cubes
- 1 onion, halved
- 2 carrots, peeled and chopped
- 2 cloves garlic, minced
- 4 cups chicken broth
- 1 bouquet garni (thyme, bay leaf, parsley)
- 1/2 cup heavy cream
- 1/4 cup flour
- 2 tbsp butter
- Salt and pepper to taste

Instructions:

1. In a large pot, melt butter over medium heat. Add veal cubes and brown them on all sides, about 8 minutes.
2. Add the onion, carrots, and garlic to the pot and cook for 5 minutes.
3. Sprinkle the flour over the meat and vegetables, then stir well to coat. Gradually add the chicken broth, stirring constantly to avoid lumps.
4. Add the bouquet garni, salt, and pepper. Bring to a simmer, cover, and cook for 1.5-2 hours, until the veal is tender.
5. Remove the bouquet garni and stir in the heavy cream. Adjust seasoning with salt and pepper.
6. Serve hot with rice or potatoes.

Entrecôte Bordelaise (Ribeye Steak with Red Wine Sauce)

Ingredients:

- 4 ribeye steaks
- 1 tbsp olive oil
- 2 tbsp butter
- 1 onion, chopped
- 1 cup red wine (preferably Bordeaux)
- 1 cup beef broth
- 2 tbsp fresh parsley, chopped
- Salt and pepper to taste

Instructions:

1. Season the ribeye steaks with salt and pepper. Heat olive oil in a skillet over high heat.
2. Sear the steaks for 4-5 minutes per side for medium-rare, or to your desired doneness. Remove from the pan and set aside to rest.
3. In the same skillet, add butter and sauté the onion until soft, about 5 minutes.
4. Add the red wine and beef broth, scraping up any browned bits from the bottom of the skillet. Bring to a simmer and cook for 10-12 minutes, until the sauce has reduced by half.
5. Stir in the fresh parsley and season with salt and pepper.
6. Serve the steaks with the sauce poured over the top.

Pâtisserie Mille-Feuille (Napoleon)

Ingredients:

- 1 package puff pastry (store-bought or homemade)
- 1 cup pastry cream (recipe below)
- 1/4 cup powdered sugar for dusting
- 1 tbsp dark chocolate, melted (optional)

Pastry Cream:

- 1 cup whole milk
- 2 large egg yolks
- 1/4 cup sugar
- 2 tbsp cornstarch
- 1 tsp vanilla extract
- 2 tbsp butter

Instructions:

1. Preheat your oven to 400°F (200°C). Roll out the puff pastry on a floured surface and cut into 3 rectangles of equal size.
2. Bake the pastry for 12-15 minutes, or until golden and puffed. Let it cool completely.
3. While the pastry cools, make the pastry cream by whisking together the egg yolks, sugar, cornstarch, and milk. Heat in a saucepan until it thickens, then remove from heat and stir in vanilla and butter. Let cool.
4. Once the pastry is cool, cut each rectangle in half to form 6 layers of pastry.
5. Spread a layer of pastry cream between two layers of pastry, then top with another layer of pastry.
6. Dust the top layer with powdered sugar and drizzle with melted chocolate if desired. Serve chilled.

Crêpes Suzette

Ingredients:

- 8 crêpes (see basic crêpes recipe below)
- 1/4 cup unsalted butter
- 1/4 cup orange juice
- 2 tbsp orange zest
- 1/4 cup Grand Marnier (or other orange liqueur)
- 1/4 cup sugar

Crêpes:

- 1 cup flour
- 2 eggs
- 1 cup milk
- 2 tbsp melted butter
- Pinch of salt

Instructions:

1. Make the crêpes: whisk together the flour, eggs, milk, melted butter, and salt to form a smooth batter. Heat a non-stick skillet over medium heat and cook the crêpes one at a time, flipping once golden brown on each side.
2. In a separate pan, melt the butter over medium heat. Add the orange juice, zest, Grand Marnier, and sugar, stirring until the sugar dissolves and the sauce thickens slightly.
3. Place the crêpes in the pan, folding each one into quarters. Let them soak in the sauce for a minute, then flip to coat the other side.
4. Serve the crêpes immediately, spooning the sauce over the top.

Crème Brûlée

Ingredients:

- 2 cups heavy cream
- 1 vanilla bean (or 1 tsp vanilla extract)
- 5 large egg yolks
- 1/2 cup sugar, plus extra for caramelizing
- Pinch of salt

Instructions:

1. Preheat your oven to 325°F (160°C). Place ramekins in a baking dish and set aside.
2. In a saucepan, heat the heavy cream over medium heat with the vanilla bean (or extract). Bring to a simmer, then remove from heat and let it sit for 10 minutes.
3. In a separate bowl, whisk together egg yolks, sugar, and salt. Gradually add the warm cream to the egg mixture, whisking constantly to prevent curdling.
4. Pour the custard mixture into the ramekins, filling them about 3/4 full. Add hot water to the baking dish to reach halfway up the sides of the ramekins.
5. Bake for 40-45 minutes, until the custard is set but still slightly wobbly.
6. Chill the custards in the refrigerator for at least 2 hours.
7. Before serving, sprinkle a thin layer of sugar on top of each custard and caramelize with a kitchen torch until golden and crisp.

Pot-au-Feu (French Boiled Beef Stew)

Ingredients:

- 2 lbs beef shank or chuck, cut into large pieces
- 4 carrots, peeled and cut into chunks
- 2 leeks, cleaned and cut into halves
- 2 onions, halved
- 4 cloves garlic, smashed
- 1 bouquet garni (parsley, thyme, and bay leaves tied together)
- 10 small potatoes, unpeeled
- Salt and pepper to taste
- 6 cups beef broth
- 1/2 tsp mustard seeds (optional)

Instructions:

1. In a large pot, add the beef, carrots, leeks, onions, garlic, bouquet garni, and mustard seeds if using.
2. Cover with beef broth and bring to a boil. Skim off any foam that rises to the top.
3. Reduce the heat, cover, and simmer for 2.5 to 3 hours, until the beef is tender.
4. Add the potatoes and cook for another 30 minutes, until they are tender.
5. Remove the beef and vegetables from the pot, and strain the broth if desired.
6. Serve the beef and vegetables with some of the broth on the side, and mustard or horseradish if preferred.

Hachis Parmentier (French Shepherd's Pie)

Ingredients:

- 1 lb ground beef or leftover cooked beef, shredded
- 2 cups mashed potatoes (preferably leftover)
- 1 onion, chopped
- 2 cloves garlic, minced
- 1 cup beef broth
- 1/4 cup red wine (optional)
- 1/2 tsp thyme
- 1 tbsp butter
- Salt and pepper to taste
- 1/2 cup grated Gruyère cheese (optional)

Instructions:

1. In a large skillet, melt butter over medium heat and sauté the onion and garlic until soft.
2. Add the ground beef (or shredded leftover beef) and cook until browned. Add the red wine (if using) and let it reduce for a few minutes.
3. Stir in the beef broth and thyme. Simmer for 10 minutes until the mixture thickens and is well combined. Season with salt and pepper.
4. Preheat the oven to 375°F (190°C).
5. In a baking dish, spread the beef mixture evenly. Top with mashed potatoes, smoothing them out with a spatula. If desired, sprinkle the grated Gruyère cheese on top.
6. Bake for 20 minutes until the top is golden and crispy.
7. Serve hot and enjoy.

Cassoulet Toulousain (Toulouse-Style Cassoulet)

Ingredients:

- 1 lb white beans (such as Great Northern or Tarbais beans), soaked overnight
- 2 tablespoons olive oil
- 1 lb pork shoulder, cut into chunks
- 4 Toulouse sausages (or any rustic French sausage)
- 2 duck legs confit (or 4 chicken thighs)
- 1 onion, chopped
- 3 cloves garlic, minced
- 2 tomatoes, chopped
- 1 bouquet garni (thyme, parsley, bay leaves)
- 4 cups chicken broth
- Salt and pepper to taste
- 1/2 cup breadcrumbs (optional)

Instructions:

1. Drain and rinse the soaked beans. In a large pot, cook them in salted water for about 1 hour, or until tender. Drain and set aside.
2. In a large, heavy pot or Dutch oven, heat olive oil over medium heat. Brown the pork shoulder chunks on all sides, then remove them from the pot and set aside.
3. In the same pot, brown the sausages and duck legs, then remove and set aside.
4. Add the onion and garlic to the pot and sauté for 5 minutes until softened. Add the tomatoes and cook for another 5 minutes.
5. Return the pork, sausages, and duck to the pot. Add the cooked beans, bouquet garni, and chicken broth. Bring to a simmer, then cover and cook for 2-3 hours, checking occasionally.
6. Preheat the oven to 375°F (190°C). If desired, sprinkle the top with breadcrumbs and bake for 30-40 minutes until the cassoulet is golden and bubbling.
7. Serve hot with crusty bread.

Pâté de Campagne (Country Pâté)

Ingredients:

- 1 lb ground pork
- 1/2 lb pork liver, finely chopped
- 1/2 lb fatty bacon, chopped
- 1 small onion, finely chopped
- 2 cloves garlic, minced
- 1/2 cup dry white wine
- 1/4 tsp thyme
- 1/4 tsp ground nutmeg
- 1/4 tsp allspice
- Salt and pepper to taste
- 2 tbsp fresh parsley, chopped
- 1 egg
- 1/4 cup heavy cream
- 2 tbsp cognac or brandy (optional)

Instructions:

1. In a large bowl, combine all the ingredients. Mix well with your hands to ensure an even distribution of spices and herbs.
2. Transfer the mixture to a loaf pan or terrine, pressing it down to eliminate air pockets.
3. Cover with foil and bake at 350°F (175°C) for 1.5 to 2 hours. The pâté is done when it reaches an internal temperature of 160°F (71°C).
4. Allow to cool at room temperature, then refrigerate for several hours or overnight before serving.
5. Serve sliced with crusty bread or pickles.

Salade de Foie de Volaille (Chicken Liver Salad)

Ingredients:

- 1 lb chicken livers, trimmed
- 1 tbsp olive oil
- 1 small shallot, finely chopped
- 1 tbsp brandy (optional)
- 4 cups mixed salad greens (e.g., arugula, lettuce, or watercress)
- 2 tbsp red wine vinegar
- 2 tbsp olive oil
- 1/2 tsp Dijon mustard
- Salt and pepper to taste
- 1/4 cup croutons (optional)

Instructions:

1. Heat the olive oil in a skillet over medium-high heat. Add the chicken livers and sauté for 4-5 minutes on each side, until browned and cooked through. Add the shallots during the last minute and cook until softened.
2. Add the brandy (if using) to the skillet, scraping up any bits stuck to the pan. Cook for another 1-2 minutes until the alcohol evaporates.
3. In a small bowl, whisk together red wine vinegar, olive oil, mustard, salt, and pepper to make the dressing.
4. Toss the salad greens with the dressing. Top with the sautéed chicken livers and shallots, and garnish with croutons if desired.
5. Serve immediately.

Gratin de Courgettes (Zucchini Gratin)

Ingredients:

- 4 medium zucchinis, thinly sliced
- 1 onion, chopped
- 1/2 cup grated Gruyère cheese
- 1/4 cup breadcrumbs
- 2 tbsp butter
- 1/2 cup heavy cream
- Salt and pepper to taste
- Fresh thyme (optional)

Instructions:

1. Preheat the oven to 375°F (190°C).
2. In a large skillet, melt the butter and sauté the onions until translucent. Add the zucchini slices and cook for 5-7 minutes until softened. Season with salt and pepper.
3. Transfer the zucchini and onions to a greased baking dish. Pour the cream over the top and sprinkle with cheese and breadcrumbs.
4. Bake for 20-25 minutes, or until the top is golden and bubbly. Garnish with fresh thyme if desired.
5. Serve hot.

Oeufs en Cocotte (Eggs in Pots)

Ingredients:

- 4 eggs
- 4 tbsp heavy cream
- 1 tbsp butter
- 4 tsp grated cheese (Gruyère or Parmesan)
- Salt and pepper to taste
- Fresh herbs (e.g., chives or parsley)

Instructions:

1. Preheat your oven to 375°F (190°C).
2. Grease 4 small ramekins with butter. Crack an egg into each ramekin.
3. Add 1 tablespoon of cream to each ramekin, and sprinkle with salt, pepper, and cheese.
4. Place the ramekins in a baking dish and add hot water to the baking dish until it reaches halfway up the sides of the ramekins.
5. Bake for 12-15 minutes, or until the eggs are set but the yolks are still runny.
6. Serve immediately, garnished with fresh herbs.

Tarte Flambée (Alsatian Pizza)

Ingredients:

- 1 package pizza dough (or homemade dough)
- 1/2 cup crème fraîche
- 1/2 cup ricotta cheese
- 1 onion, thinly sliced
- 6 oz lardons (or bacon), chopped
- Salt and pepper to taste
- 1/2 cup grated Gruyère cheese

Instructions:

1. Preheat the oven to 475°F (245°C).
2. Roll out the pizza dough on a floured surface into a thin rectangle or circle.
3. Mix the crème fraîche and ricotta cheese together, then spread evenly over the dough.
4. Top with sliced onions, lardons, and grated cheese.
5. Bake for 10-12 minutes until the dough is crisp and the toppings are golden.
6. Slice and serve immediately.

Vichyssoise (Cold Leek and Potato Soup)

Ingredients:

- 4 large leeks, cleaned and chopped (white and light green parts only)
- 2 medium potatoes, peeled and diced
- 1 small onion, chopped
- 4 cups chicken or vegetable stock
- 1/2 cup heavy cream
- 2 tbsp butter
- Salt and pepper to taste
- Fresh chives for garnish

Instructions:

1. In a large pot, melt butter over medium heat. Add the leeks and onion, cooking until softened (about 5 minutes).
2. Add the potatoes and stock to the pot. Bring to a boil, then reduce the heat and simmer for about 20 minutes, until the potatoes are tender.
3. Remove from heat and let the soup cool slightly. Using an immersion blender, blend the soup until smooth. You can also transfer it to a blender in batches.
4. Stir in the cream and season with salt and pepper to taste.
5. Chill the soup in the refrigerator for at least 2 hours before serving.
6. Serve cold, garnished with fresh chives.

Soufflé au Fromage (Cheese Soufflé)

Ingredients:

- 2 tbsp butter
- 2 tbsp flour
- 1 cup whole milk
- 1 1/2 cups grated Gruyère cheese (or a mix of Gruyère and Emmental)
- 4 large eggs, separated
- Salt and pepper to taste
- A pinch of cayenne pepper (optional)
- 1/4 tsp mustard powder (optional)

Instructions:

1. Preheat the oven to 375°F (190°C). Grease a soufflé dish with butter and dust with flour.
2. In a saucepan, melt butter over medium heat. Stir in the flour and cook for 1-2 minutes to form a roux.
3. Gradually whisk in the milk, stirring continuously until the mixture thickens. Remove from heat and stir in the cheese until melted and smooth.
4. Stir in the egg yolks, salt, pepper, cayenne, and mustard powder (if using).
5. In a separate bowl, whisk the egg whites until stiff peaks form. Gently fold the egg whites into the cheese mixture until combined.
6. Pour the mixture into the prepared soufflé dish, smooth the top, and bake for 25-30 minutes, until golden and puffed.
7. Serve immediately.

Salade de Langoustines (Langoustine Salad)

Ingredients:

- 12 langoustines (or shrimp if langoustines are unavailable)
- 4 cups mixed salad greens (e.g., arugula, watercress)
- 1 avocado, sliced
- 1 small cucumber, sliced
- 1/2 red onion, thinly sliced
- 1/4 cup olive oil
- 2 tbsp lemon juice
- Salt and pepper to taste
- Fresh parsley for garnish

Instructions:

1. Boil the langoustines in salted water for 3-4 minutes until pink and cooked through. Drain and let cool.
2. Once cooled, peel the langoustines and set aside.
3. In a large bowl, combine the mixed greens, avocado, cucumber, and red onion.
4. In a small bowl, whisk together the olive oil, lemon juice, salt, and pepper.
5. Toss the salad with the dressing, then top with the langoustines.
6. Garnish with fresh parsley and serve.

Brandade de Morue (Salt Cod Brandade)

Ingredients:

- 1 lb salt cod, soaked overnight and shredded
- 2 large potatoes, peeled and boiled
- 1/2 cup olive oil
- 3 cloves garlic, minced
- 1/4 cup heavy cream
- Salt and pepper to taste
- Fresh parsley for garnish

Instructions:

1. In a large pot, cover the salt cod with water and bring to a boil. Simmer for about 10 minutes, then drain and let it cool slightly. Remove the skin and bones, then shred the fish.
2. Mash the boiled potatoes in a bowl.
3. In a skillet, heat the olive oil over medium heat and sauté the garlic until fragrant, about 1 minute.
4. Add the shredded salt cod and mashed potatoes to the skillet, stirring to combine. Slowly add the olive oil and cream, mixing until the brandade is smooth and creamy.
5. Season with salt and pepper to taste.
6. Transfer to a serving dish and garnish with fresh parsley. Serve warm with crusty bread.

Gâteau Basque (Basque Cake)

Ingredients:

- **For the Pastry:**
    - 2 1/2 cups all-purpose flour
    - 1 cup butter, softened
    - 1 cup sugar
    - 2 large eggs
    - 1/2 tsp vanilla extract
    - 1/2 tsp almond extract
    - 1/4 tsp salt
    - 1 tsp baking powder
- **For the Filling:**
    - 1 cup pastry cream (prepared in advance, recipe below)
    - OR 1/2 cup cherry jam (optional)

Instructions:

1. Preheat the oven to 350°F (175°C). Grease and flour a round cake pan.
2. In a mixing bowl, combine the flour, sugar, baking powder, and salt. Add the butter and mix until the dough comes together.
3. Add the eggs, vanilla, and almond extract, and mix to form a smooth dough.
4. Roll out about two-thirds of the dough and line the bottom and sides of the prepared pan.
5. Fill with pastry cream (or cherry jam for a variation), then roll out the remaining dough and cover the filling.
6. Bake for 35-40 minutes, or until the cake is golden brown.
7. Let cool before serving.

For the Pastry Cream:

- 1 1/4 cups milk
- 1/2 cup sugar
- 3 large egg yolks
- 2 tbsp cornstarch
- 1 tsp vanilla extract

Instructions for Pastry Cream:

1. In a saucepan, heat the milk until simmering.
2. In a separate bowl, whisk the egg yolks, sugar, and cornstarch until smooth.
3. Slowly pour the hot milk into the egg mixture, whisking constantly. Return the mixture to the pan and cook over medium heat until it thickens.
4. Remove from heat and stir in the vanilla extract. Let cool.

Pain Complet (Whole Wheat Bread)

Ingredients:

- 3 cups whole wheat flour
- 1 cup all-purpose flour
- 1 1/2 tsp salt
- 1 tsp sugar
- 1 tbsp dry yeast
- 1 1/4 cups warm water
- 2 tbsp olive oil

Instructions:

1. In a large bowl, mix the whole wheat flour, all-purpose flour, salt, and sugar.
2. In a separate bowl, dissolve the yeast in warm water and let sit for 5 minutes until foamy.
3. Add the yeast mixture and olive oil to the flour mixture. Stir until the dough forms.
4. Knead the dough on a floured surface for about 8-10 minutes until smooth and elastic.
5. Place the dough in a greased bowl, cover, and let rise for 1 hour.
6. Punch down the dough, shape it into a loaf, and place it in a greased loaf pan.
7. Preheat the oven to 375°F (190°C). Bake the bread for 30-35 minutes until golden brown and hollow when tapped on the bottom.
8. Let cool before slicing.

Pain de Campagne (French Country Bread)

Ingredients:

- 4 cups all-purpose flour
- 1 1/2 tsp salt
- 1 tsp dry yeast
- 1 1/2 cups warm water
- 1 tbsp olive oil

Instructions:

1. In a large bowl, combine the flour and salt.
2. In a small bowl, dissolve the yeast in warm water and let sit for 5 minutes.
3. Add the yeast mixture and olive oil to the flour mixture, stirring to form a dough.
4. Knead the dough on a floured surface for about 10 minutes until smooth and elastic.
5. Place the dough in a greased bowl, cover with a damp cloth, and let rise for 1-2 hours, or until doubled in size.
6. Punch down the dough, shape it into a round loaf, and place on a baking sheet.
7. Preheat the oven to 400°F (200°C). Bake the bread for 30-35 minutes until golden and hollow when tapped.
8. Let cool before slicing.

www.ingramcontent.com/pod-product-compliance
Lightning Source LLC
LaVergne TN
LVHW081500060526
838201LV00056BA/2843